THE PEASANT Prince

THE PLAY
BASED ON THE BOOK BY LI CUNXIN

Adapted by
Eva Di Cesare,
Sandra Eldridge
and Tim McGarry

CURRENCY PRESS
SYDNEY

CURRENCY PRESS

First published in 2018
by Currency Press Pty Ltd,
Gadigal Land, Suite 310, 46–56 Kippax Street, Surry Hills, NSW 2010, Australia
enquiries@currency.com.au
www.currency.com.au

Cataloguing-in-publication data for this title is available from the National Library of Australia website: www.nla.gov.au

Typeset for Currency Press by Dean Nottle.
Cover design by Studio Emma for Currency Press.

Currency Press acknowledges the Traditional Owners of the Country on which we live and work. We pay our respects to all Aboriginal and Torres Strait Islander Elders, past and present.

CONTENTS

John Gomez Goodway as Li Cunxin in Monkey Baa's 2016 production. (Photo: Heidrun Löhr)

ABOUT LI CUNXIN

Li was born in 1961 into utter poverty in Mao's communist China. At the age of 11, he was selected to train in Madame Mao's Beijing Dance Academy. And so began Li's journey. The seven-year harsh training regime at the Academy taught him discipline, resilience, determination and perseverance. Li's astounding drive and relentless hard work made him one of the best dancers China has ever produced.

When he was 18, Li was awarded one of the first cultural scholarships to study in America. Li then defected to the West in a dramatic media storm which involved the then- Vice President, George Bush Snr. He went on to become a principal dancer of Houston Ballet and one of the best dancers in the world, winning two silver medals and a bronze medal over three International Ballet Competitions. In 1995, Li and his family moved to Australia where Li danced his last three-and-a-half years as a principal artist with the Australian Ballet.

For the final two years of his dancing, Li studied finance at the Australian Securities Institute with a view of becoming a stockbroker. This meant rising at five in the morning to start his daily ballet practice, then racing to the stock exchange by eight. By the time he joined the rest of the company's dancers for afternoon rehearsals, he had already put in a full day's work. Li made a successful career transition from ballet to finance in 1999. He was a senior manager at one of the largest stockbroking firms in Australia. In 2013, Li became Artistic Director of Queensland Ballet.

The rich story of Li's inspirational life is recounted in his memoir *Mao's Last Dancer*, which was published in September 2003. It quickly rose to number one on the Australian non-fiction bestseller list and was named in Amazon's Break-Out Books list within weeks of its US release. The memoir received the Christopher Award for Literature and the Australian Book of the Year Award, and was shortlisted for several other prestigious literary awards. Li's book has been translated into several foreign languages and is sold in over 20 countries worldwide.

Academy Award winning director Bruce Beresford, producer Jane Scott and screenwriter Jan Sardi teamed up to produce a feature film based on Li's extraordinary life. It was released in 2009 to critical acclaim.

Li received the Shepherd Centre's Australian Father of the Year Award in 2009, and has been honoured with a doctorate for his contribution to arts and literature by the Australian Catholic University. Li was named Queensland Australian of the Year in 2014 and received the Asia Society's Game Changer Award in 2015.

ABOUT MONKEY BAA THEATRE COMPANY

Eva Di Cesare, Sandra Eldridge and Tim McGarry

Three actors sitting in a Darlinghurst coffee shop on a wet and windy April morning in 1997 seems an unlikely scenario for the birth of a theatre company, but that's exactly where the seeds of Monkey Baa were first sown. During its first tour of *The Bugalugs Bum Thief* (adapted from the book by Tim Winton) in 1998 in a long wheelbase van, the cast lugged a heavy set into classrooms, libraries and community halls across Australia, performing to over 15,000 young people. And with that Monkey Baa Theatre Company was born.

Since then, we have been creating inspiring, award-winning theatre for young audiences. Our Creative Directors have adapted over 15 classic Australian stories for the stage, with a common thread throughout that respects and values young people's interests. We believe Australian stages should be filled with stories that represent all the extraordinary cultures living in this land, and that it's important to create work that offers young people a truly multifaceted reflection of the world we all inhabit. Unlike other theatre companies offering work for young audiences, we take a 'whole of childhood' approach, creating plays and arts education programs for ages three to eighteen and providing professional development opportunities for teachers. We strive to ensure that young people, wherever they are located and whatever their economic circumstances, have the opportunity to share in fantastic theatre experiences that reflect their own lives.

One of Australia's largest touring companies, Monkey Baa has conducted over 25 national tours to 135 regional and remote communities across every state and territory of Australia, four international tours and over 2,500 performances, and engaged with 1.2 million young people. As resident company at the Lendlease Darling Quarter Theatre, we curate an annual season of theatre for young people in school holidays and term time, presenting Monkey Baa plays and work from other Australian and international companies.

Mission Statement

To share uniquely Australian stories, with young people at the heart of everything we create.

Vision Statement

To be a company that exhilarates young minds and reveals a world of infinite possibilities; a place where theatre becomes an intrinsic part of a young person's life.

DIRECTOR'S NOTE

This is your lucky chance to escape from this cruel world. Become someone other than a peasant boy. I know you have your secret dreams. Follow them. Make them come true. —Niang, Li's mother

I remember being completely captivated by Li's remarkable story when I first read *Mao's Last Dancer* in 2003. In 2012 a small rural school in Home Hill, Queensland, acted out a section of *The Peasant Prince* in a drama workshop. Little did these students realise their love of young Cunxin's story would grab the attention of Monkey Baa, who would then go on to create a new theatre work for young audiences everywhere to enjoy.

Li Cunxin's life journey feels like a fairytale, a rags-to-riches story about a boy who was propelled from a life of poverty onto the world stage, to become one of the greatest ballet dancers of our time. It is all of this and so much more—a story of fate and agency, pain and loneliness, an astonishingly determined spirit to overcome adversity, an emotional and physical struggle to simply survive.

In many respects Li's journey is a series of migrations—a story of travelling across the world to seek new opportunity. A story the majority of Australians are all too familiar with, be it a recent family migration or many generations before—those who took similar risks for a better life. Li Cunxin, we salute you and thank you for reminding us that it takes courage and sacrifice to make that almighty leap out of the well. You are an inspiration and we are indebted to you for entrusting us with your story.

Tim McGarry
Director, Monkey Baa Theatre Company

ACKNOWLEDGEMENTS

Monkey Baa Theatre Company gratefully acknowledges all who supported *The Peasant Prince* including:

- Annette Shun Wah and Performance 4A
- Ming Liang and the Australia China Relations Institute
- Professor Stephanie Hemelryk Donald FASSA FRSA

The development of *The Peasant Prince* was supported by a Rex Cramphorn Residency at the Department of Theatre and Performance Studies, University of Sydney.

Eva, Sandie and Tim wish to especially thank Li Cunxin, for his extraordinary support and passion for the project, and for his story.

The Peasant Prince was first produced by Monkey Baa Theatre Company at the Lendlease Darling Quarter Theatre, Sydney, on 9 April 2016, with the following cast:

LI CUNXIN   John Gomez Goodway

DIA / CONSUL ZHANG / TEACHER CHEN YUEN /
TEACHER XIAO / UNCLE   Jonathan Chan

NIANG / AUNTY / CLARE DUNCAN /
TEACHER GAO / TEACHER SONG   Jenevieve Chang

CUNFAR / BEN STEVENSON /
TEACHER CHEN LUENG / WANG LU JUN   Edric Hong

Minor roles were shared between the actors.

Director, Tim McGarry
Movement Director, Danielle Micich (courtesy of Force Majeure)
Set & Costume Designer, Michael Hankin
Lighting Designer, Sian James-Holland
Sound Designer, Daryl Wallis
Audiovisual Designer, David Bergman
Script Consultant, Li Cunxin
Dramaturge, Camilla Ah Kin
Production Manager, Cally Bartley
Production Coordinator, Damion Holling
Set & Costume Design Assistant, Charlie Davis
Costume Maker, Leah Giblin
Stage Manager, Kelly Ukena
Technical Coordinator, Russell Stewart

Characters

LI CUNXIN [*pronounced: Lee Schwin-Sing*]

DIA, Cunxin's father
NIANG, Cunxin's mother
CUNFAR, one of Cunxin's brothers
UNCLE
AUNTY
TEACHER SONG, Cunxin's teacher in the village
LING WEI, a student in the village
STUDENTS in the village

OFFICIALS [2]
TEACHER CHEN LUENG, a ballet academy teacher
TEACHER CHEN YUEN, a ballet academy teacher
TEACHER GAO, a ballet academy teacher
TEACHER XIAO, Cunxin's favourite teacher and mentor
WANG LU JUN ('The Bandit'), Cunxin's friend

BEN STEVENSON, Director of the Houston Ballet
CLARE DUNCAN, President of the Houston Ballet
CONSUL ZHANG, the Chinese Consulate in Houston
GUARDS [2], the Chinese Consulate in Houston
JANICE, Radio Houston [*voiceover*]
STAGE MANAGER of the Houston Ballet

Setting

The play opens in America, where Li Cunxin as an adult prepares to perform for the Houston Ballet in *The Nutcracker*. As Cunxin prepares to perform, his memory takes the audience back to his childhood in Qingdao, his small rural village in northern China.

We then see Cunxin at the age of eleven, training hard in Beijing after being selected for Madame Mao's Dance Academy. His life changes forever.

One day a famous ballet master visits the Beijing Academy from the USA. We then follow Cunxin and the ballet master to Houston, eventually ending up at the scene where we started. The young man who becomes a famous dancer will always remember himself as a small boy, flying his kite on a bitterly cold day, in a faraway place called Qingdao.

Chairman Mao's image is on a screen at the back of the stage as the audience enters.

Prologue

Houston, Texas.

We hear the foyer bells and the orchestra warming up, indicating a show is about to begin. **LI CUNXIN** *is in position, ready.*

We hear a voiceover making the audience announcement: 'Ladies and gentlemen, in tonight's performance of Houston Ballet's The Nutcracker, *the role of the Prince will be danced by Li Cunxin.'*

The **STAGE MANAGER** *enters, talking into a cordless radio microphone pack.*

STAGE MANAGER: I'm still waiting for clearance. Li, your parents have finally arrived.

CUNXIN: Where are they sitting?

STAGE MANAGER: [*on the mic*] Where are they seated? The parents? [*To* **CUNXIN**] Front row centre.

CUNXIN: I haven't seen my Niang and my Dia in six years.

STAGE MANAGER: They'll be so proud. Li, we have Front of House clearance, are you ready? You are the Prince. [*On the mic*] Ladies and gentlemen of the company, please stand by.

>   *The* **STAGE MANAGER** *exits.*
>
>   *We hear the opening bars of 'The Nutcracker Suite'.*
>
>   *We transition into* **CUNXIN**'s *memory. We hear children from his classroom singing and the echo of* **NIANG** *and* **DIA**'s *voices*

1

from the past. **NIANG** *and* **DIA** *appear.*

NIANG: *Bie hwai to. Bu yao yong yuen two yi ge no ming.* Don't look back. Become someone other than a peasant boy.

DIA: *Gang so dao feng le ma, Cunxin.* Feel the current of the wind, Cunxin.

NIANG: I know you have your secret dreams. Follow them.

DIA: Like a bird, go with the current of the wind.

NIANG: *Jio zwai swag le ta men.* Follow them … Follow them.

> *We hear the flapping of a kite.*

Scene One

On the fields of Shandong Province. Winter.

CUNXIN *flies the kite as* **DIA** *looks on.* **NIANG** *is observing her husband and son as she folds a blanket.*

CUNXIN: Dia, look! Look how high it's flying.

DIA: Keep moving, Cunxin, keep your arms moving … That's it, son. Keep moving.

> *We hear the wind getting stronger.* **CUNXIN** *begins to lose control of the kite.*

Pull to the right, no Cunxin, more to the right.

CUNXIN: Dia, Dia … no …

> *The kite crashes in the field.* **CUNXIN** *runs to the broken kite. He is distraught.*

Dia, it's broken.

DIA: You need to feel the current of the wind, Cunxin, like a bird, go with the current of the wind.

CUNXIN: Can you fix it?

Jonathan Chan as Dia and John Gomez Goodway as Li Cunxin in Monkey Baa's 2016 production. (Photo: Heidrun Löhr)

DIA: I've got my work to do. I'll fix it later.

CUNXIN: Can you fix it now? Please Dia? Please?

> **DIA** *reluctantly begins to fix the kite.*

DIA: Give me the kite.

CUNXIN: Thank you, Dia. Can you tell me a story?

DIA: Now you're asking for too much.

CUNXIN: Please?

DIA: I've told you all the stories I have.

CUNXIN: Once upon a time, there was a frog that lived in a deep, dark well.

> **CUNXIN** *hops around his* **DIA**, *trying to encourage him to tell the story.*

DIA: Alright, alright, I'll tell you. Once upon a time, there was a frog that lived in a deep dark well.

CUNXIN: Ribbit.

DIA: It was the only home he knew. One day he met a frog who lived in the world above.

CUNXIN: 'Come down and play with me.' Ribbit.

DIA: 'My world up here is much bigger!' So the frog in the well went and told his father what he'd heard.

CUNXIN: Ribbit.

DIA: 'My son,' his father said, 'I've heard there is a bigger and better world up there. But your destiny is down here in the well. There is no way you can get out.'

CUNXIN: 'I can, I can get out of here. Let me show you.'

DIA: 'It's no use, my son. Forget the world above. Be satisfied with what you have.'

CUNXIN: 'I want to get out. I want to see the big world above.'

DIA: 'My son. You must accept fate. Learn to live with what is …'

BOTH: [*together*] '… given.'

CUNXIN: Dia, are we in a well?

DIA: Depends on how you look at it, Cunxin. If you look at where we are from heaven above, yes, we're in a well. But if you look at us from below, we're not in a well.

CUNXIN: Are we in heaven, Dia?

DIA: No. Definitely not.

> **DIA** *has finished fixing the kite.*

Here you go. Enough stories, I have to get to work and you need to get to school. Pray to the gods it will fly.

CUNXIN: Thanks, Dia.

> **DIA** *exits.* **CUNXIN** *pulls paper strips out of his pocket, and ties them to the kite for each wish.*

For my first wish, I wish for my Dia's good health. My father works so hard for us all.

For my second wish, I wish for my Niang's happiness and long life. My mother is the kindest, most hard-working Niang. She deserves better.

For my last wish—the most important wish of all … get me out of this deep dark well so I can help my family.

> *We hear the wind.*

> **CUNXIN** *exits, flying his kite, with his three wishes attached.*

Scene Two

In the school classroom. We hear a school bell. We hear the Chinese national anthem. There is an image of Chairman Mao on the wall.

The **STUDENTS,** *including* **CUNXIN,** *march into class singing the*

Chinese national anthem and waving their little red books. **TEACHER SONG** *steps forward.*

TEACHER SONG: Good morning, students.

STUDENTS: Good morning, Teacher Song.

TEACHER SONG: We wish Chairman Mao a long, long life because our Great Leader saved us. He is our saviour, our sun, our moon.

STUDENTS: Long live Chairman Mao! I love Chairman Mao!

TEACHER SONG: Children like you couldn't even dream of sitting here in the classroom, but our beloved Chairman Mao has made it possible for everyone in China to have this privilege.

STUDENTS: Long live Chairman Mao! I love Chairman Mao!

TEACHER SONG: Have your parents told you about the cruel life they lived under Chiang Kaishek?

STUDENTS: Yes, Teacher Song!

TEACHER SONG: And who did that government care for?

STUDENTS: The filthy landlords, Teacher Song!

TEACHER SONG: They were cold, dark days indeed.

STUDENTS: Yes, Teacher Song!

TEACHER SONG: Students, today we are going to honour the inspiring stories of Lei Feng, the faithful and humble soldier of our beloved Chairman Mao.

    The **STUDENTS** *cheer excitedly.*

Bi jwai. Quiet. We all remember Lei Feng's good deeds. How have you honoured him in your daily life? What good deed have you done?

STUDENT 1: I helped an old aunty with bound feet get water from her well.

STUDENT 2: I went to an old man's home to help him sweep his yard.

CUNXIN: I picked up horse poo from the street and took it to the fields as fertiliser.

> The other **STUDENTS** *laugh.* **TEACHER SONG** *bangs a stick on the ground.*

TEACHER SONG: *Bi jwai!* Quiet! Enough! Cunxin! When did you do this deed?

CUNXIN: Yesterday, before school.

TEACHER SONG: This is a model citizen! Lei Feng would have been proud. Students, what are our beloved Chairman Mao's three 'Goods'?

STUDENTS: Good study! Good work! Good health!

> We hear the school bell ring.

Scene Three

On the way home. **CUNXIN** *and* **CUNFAR.**

CUNFAR: I hate school. What a boring day. I'm glad we didn't do mathematics, Sixth Brother. I hate mathematics.

CUNXIN: I hate Chinese, Fifth Brother. When Teacher Song writes it on the board most of it looks like grass to me.

CUNFAR: That's what I first thought, but it gets better.

CUNXIN: I don't believe you. What's the use of learning words anyway?

CUNFAR: I don't know.

CUNXIN: How will being a clever student make me a good peasant?

CUNFAR: I don't know.

CUNXIN: How will school help us get more food?

CUNFAR: I don't know.

CUNXIN: The best bit is the stories about Lei Feng.

CUNFAR *neighs like a horse, mimics the horse pooing and directs* **CUNXIN** *to pick it up.*

CUNFAR: Do your good deed. Pick up my poo.

CUNXIN: I'm going to kill you.

CUNXIN *chases* **CUNFAR** *and they arrive at the family compound, fighting.*

CUNFAR: Niang! Sixth Brother is trying to kill me.

NIANG *comes out from the house.*

NIANG: What are you both doing?

CUNXIN: Fifth Brother is making fun of me.

NIANG: Cunfar, get to the field and help your Dia dig for yams.

CUNFAR *exits with a little 'neigh'.* **NIANG** *pulls a small car out of her pocket and shows it to* **CUNXIN**.

Is this your toy car?

CUNXIN *is silent.*

Get inside. Get inside now!

They move inside.

Where did you get this toy car?

CUNXIN: I found it, Niang.

NIANG: Where?

CUNXIN: In the street.

NIANG: When?

CUNXIN: Yesterday.

NIANG: Did you steal it?

CUNXIN: No, Niang.

NIANG: You did.

CUNXIN: I didn't …

NIANG: You stole this toy car.

CUNXIN: I didn't …

NIANG: I am ashamed …

CUNXIN: But Niang—

NIANG: I am ashamed of what you have done. Push the windbox. I have tried to teach all my seven sons never to steal. Push the windbox. You have shamed me …

CUNXIN: Alright.

NIANG: You have shamed your Dia …

CUNXIN: Alright.

NIANG: You have shamed the Li family name.

CUNXIN: Alright, I stole it. But stop yelling at me!

NIANG: Push the windbox. And tomorrow you are going to return this toy.

DIA *enters from the fields and overhears* NIANG *and* CUNXIN.

CUNXIN: Why are we so poor?

NIANG: I don't know. We are born with a hopeless fate.

CUNXIN: Don't say that.

NIANG: The gods in heaven won't answer our prayers and even the devil below has abandoned us.

CUNXIN: Don't say that.

NIANG: I'm sorry. I'm sorry we are so poor.

DIA: We may be poor, but no matter how hard life is the Li family always has pride and dignity.

DIA *exits into the house.*

CUNXIN: I'll have enough food for you one day, Niang. I swear.

As night falls, we hear gentle instrumental music. NIANG *uses a blanket to care for her son. Firstly she uses it to symbolically depict mealtime, first as a wok and then as a table / picnic blanket on the ground. The blanket then becomes a towel, that*

9

she uses to dry **CUNXIN***'s hair before tenderly wrapping him up to keep him warm at bedtime. In this sequence we see mother and son reconcile from their argument.*

Scene Four

Bedtime.

An image appears of a wall covered in newspapers. The room is lit by a kerosene lamp, as the commune lights are turned off at 8 pm.

CUNXIN *and* **CUNFAR** *begin their nightly ritual of playing 'I spy' with the newspapers as* **NIANG** *and* **DIA** *set up the bed on the kang.*

CUNFAR: Dishonest? Dishonest? Found it! 'America is the most dishonest nation in the world!' Told you I'd find it.

CUNXIN: Oh, alright, your turn.

CUNFAR: Okay. I spy … the word for you to find is … 'enemy'.

> **CUNXIN** *spots this quickly.*

CUNXIN: Easy. Enemy … enemy … 'The filthy West is the enemy of China'. Found it. My turn. I spy … the word for you to find is … 'greatness'.

CUNFAR: Greatness … greatness … found it! Fastest find! 'China is the source of all greatness.' Yes. Okay. Turn away. I spy … mmm … find the word 'disease'.

CUNXIN: Disease. Okay … disease … disease …

NIANG: Come on. Get into bed. Your Dia has to get up at five a.m.

CUNXIN: I've just got to find the word disease, Niang.

CUNFAR: You'll never find it.

> **CUNFAR** *gets into bed.* **CUNXIN** *is still looking for the word.*

NIANG: Cunxin, lights are going out now.

CUNXIN: Found it! 'America is dark and full of disease'. Yes! Disease. Found it!

    CUNXIN *gets into bed.*

CUNFAR: I'll give you disease, Brother. Have a taste of my disease.

    CUNFAR *puts his foot in* **CUNXIN**'s *face.*

CUNXIN: Eugh … No, no, no. Niang, Dia, Fifth Brother put his foot in my mouth.

CUNFAR: Sixth Brother put his foot on my ear.

CUNXIN: Fifth Brother kicked me.

CUNFAR: Sixth Brother stinks. Phwoaa. Cunxin.

    CUNXIN *appears from under the blanket.*

CUNXIN: It wasn't me!

DIA: Enough! Go to sleep.

    Silence.

    CUNXIN *looks out from under the blanket.*

CUNXIN: [*whispering*] It wasn't me.

Scene Five

In the school classroom. We hear the Chinese national anthem. We see the image of Chairman Mao up on the wall.

The **STUDENTS** *step forward. They chant in English and wave 'The Little Red Book'.* **TEACHER SONG** *steps forward.*

TEACHER SONG: Good morning, students.

STUDENTS: Good morning, Teacher Song.

TEACHER SONG: We wish Chairman Mao a long, long life because our Great Leader saved us. He is our saviour, our sun, our moon.

    An **OFFICIAL** *enters, wearing a Mao jacket and coat.*

STUDENTS: Long live Chairman Mao! I love Chairman Mao!

TEACHER SONG: Students, today in our school, we have a very special guest from Madame Mao's Dance Academy from Beijing. He is here to find talented students to study ballet and serve in Chairman Mao's revolution. Millions of children are being tested across China. Let us welcome our honorable guest. Ling Wei?

> TEACHER SONG *ushers* LING WEI *to the front of the classroom to sing a song for the* OFFICIAL.

LING WEI: [*sung*] *Dongfang hong, tai yang sheng*
> *Zhongguo chu liao ge Mao Ze Dong*
> *Ta wei renmin mou xingfu*
> *Hu er hai yo, ta shi ren ming da jiu xing.*

> *After* LING WEI*'s song, the* OFFICIAL *walks up and down, inspecting the* STUDENTS. *He picks out one* STUDENT.

OFFICIAL: You! Stand. We are going to test your body and your flexibility.

> *The* OFFICIAL *tests the* STUDENT*'s jumping skills.* CUNXIN *is watching with great interest.*

Stand on one leg—balance. The other leg. Balance.

> *The* STUDENT *follows the instructions. The* OFFICIAL *shouts.*

Jump for me. Higher. Higher!

> *The* OFFICIAL *begins to stretch the* STUDENT*'s leg.*

Lift. Does this hurt?

STUDENT: No.

OFFICIAL: This one?

STUDENT: No.

OFFICIAL: This one?

STUDENT: [*screaming*] *Oww!*

OFFICIAL: Thank you, that will be all.

> *The* **OFFICIAL** *goes to leave the classroom but* **TEACHER SONG** *taps him on the shoulder.*

TEACHER SONG: Excuse me, comrade? [*Indicating* **CUNXIN**] What about this one?

> *The* **OFFICIAL** *looks* **CUNXIN** *up and down and takes a moment to really take him in.*

> *The* **OFFICIAL** *then tests* **CUNXIN**.

OFFICIAL: Stand. Stand on one leg—balance. The other leg—balance.

> **CUNXIN** *follows the instructions.*

Jump for me. Higher. Higher!

> **CUNXIN** *jumps like a frog—he knows this move.*

> *The* **OFFICIAL** *stretches* **CUNXIN** *into many awkward positions.*

Lift. Does this hurt?

CUNXIN: No.

OFFICIAL: This one?

CUNXIN: No.

OFFICIAL: This one?

CUNXIN: No.

OFFICIAL: Can you go further? Further? Arms out. Out!

> *The* **OFFICIAL** *notices his scar.*

How did you get that scar?

CUNXIN: What scar?

OFFICIAL: On your arm. Do you have any sensations like itching on rainy days?

CUNXIN: No.

OFFICIAL: I've seen enough. That will be all.

From left: Jenevieve Chang as Teacher Song, John Gomez Goodway as Li Cunxin and Edric Hong as the Official in Monkey Baa's 2016 production. (Photo: Heidrun Löhr)

TEACHER SONG: *Xie xie.*

OFFICIAL: That scar will definitely get larger as he grows.

>*The **OFFICIAL** exits. **CUNXIN** and **TEACHER SONG** remain.*

Scene Six

A few months later.

CUNXIN *is at home secretly practising his ballet stretches. We hear people calling out from their homes.*

UNCLE: Hey, Cunxin, have you heard from the Beijing Academy yet?

CUNXIN: No, Fourth Uncle. No news yet.

AUNTY: *Ai-yah, Cunxin,* any news?

CUNXIN: No, Fourth Aunty. No. There's no news.

AUNTY: Well, we just have to be satisfied with what we have.

>**CUNXIN** *clocks his scar again and holds his arm.*

>**CUNFAR** *enters.*

CUNFAR: Hey, Cunxin. Show us your ballet steps.

CUNXIN: Ha ha, Fifth Brother.

CUNFAR: They bind your feet, you know.

>**NIANG** *enters.*

CUNXIN: They do not.

CUNFAR: They do. They break your toes first.

CUNXIN: Leave me alone.

CUNFAR: It's been months, Cunxin. They didn't pick you.

>**CUNXIN** *is worried.* **NIANG** *enters.*

NIANG: Enough! Cunxin, the windbox.

>**NIANG** *and* **CUNXIN** *are at the kang.* **NIANG** *is preparing food.*

CUNXIN is at the windbox.

An OFFICIAL enters.

OFFICIAL: *Ni-hao.*

NIANG: *Ning-hao.*

OFFICIAL: Are you Fang Reiqing? [*Pronounced: Fong Ri Chin*]

NIANG: I am.

OFFICIAL: The wife of Li Ting Fang?

NIANG: Yes.

OFFICIAL: Of your seven sons, which is Li Cunxin?

NIANG beckons for CUNXIN to come forward.

NIANG: Cunxin. Cunxin, *gwo lai!* This is my sixth son, Cunxin.

OFFICIAL: Fifteen children have been selected from over seventy million people. Your lucky son has been chosen for Madame Mao's Beijing Dance Academy. He has been awarded a full scholarship. He will leave for Beijing in four weeks time.

CUNFAR erupts, running off in excitement to tell the world CUNXIN's news.

CUNFAR: My brother's going to Beijing!

NIANG: *Xie xie.*

CUNFAR: My brother's going to Beijing! *Ai-yah,* my brother's going to Beijing!

NIANG falls to her knees.

NIANG: *Xie xie.* Thank you. *Xie xie.*

OFFICIAL: Congratulations. *Zai jian.*

NIANG: Thank you.

The OFFICIAL exits. NIANG and CUNXIN hug.

My lucky boy. I'm so happy for you. This is the happiest day of my life.

CUNXIN: Can you come with me to Beijing? I don't want to leave you!

NIANG: This is your lucky chance to escape from this cruel world. Become someone other than a peasant boy. I know you have your secret dreams. Follow them. Make them come true.

> **NIANG** *gives* **CUNXIN** *his handmade blanket.* **DIA** *enters with* **CUNXIN***'s netted bag with apples and shrimp inside.*

Scene Seven

Lost in Beijing Train Station. Autumn.

We hear the sounds of the busy train station with steam trains arriving and leaving. Bicycle bells. The voices of the crowds and station announcements in Mandarin.

In this movement scene **CUNXIN**, *carrying his blanket and string bag, is lost and alone in Beijing Railway Station. He is amongst a sea of people at the station, some on bicycles, all pushing and shoving, moving very fast around him, carrying sacks of produce, a man sweeping.*

He is pushed and pulled by the crowd. He looks around but doesn't know which direction to take. Exhausted and desperate, he moves to the side out of the way of the fast-moving people. He is frightened, lost, overwhelmed and alone.

Scene Eight

Beijing Dance Academy.

We hear the ballet school's bell ring. The new **STUDENTS** *listen to the voice of the director over the academy's loudspeaker: 'Students, I am*

Director Wang. On behalf of our beloved Madame Mao, welcome to the Beijing Dance Academy. You are the lucky and proud children of the workers, peasants and soldiers of China! You will carry Chairman Mao's artistic flag into the bright future.'

Ballet piano music begins as **TEACHER CHEN LUENG** *enters.*

First dance lesson.

The **STUDENTS** *line up at the barre ready to do pliés.*

TEACHER CHEN LUENG: Pliés. And one, two … This begins your six years of training.

> *Second dance lesson.*
>
> *The music changes pace.*
>
> *At the barre* **STUDENTS** *turn and face the other way.* **TEACHER CHEN YUEN** *enters.*

Hands up on the barre. Fondue. You will also study Chinese and Madame Mao's Art Philosophy.

> *Third dance lesson.*
>
> *The music changes pace, getting faster.*
>
> *The* **STUDENTS** *change positions to indicate a new class.*

TEACHER CHEN YUEN: Five, six, seven, eight. One, two, three, four. Two, two, three, four. One, two. One, two. And an in and an in and an in and an in.

> *Fourth dance lesson.*
>
> *The music changes pace again.*
>
> *The* **STUDENTS** *change positions to indicate another new class.*

TEACHER CHEN LUENG: And one, two. Higher. Higher. Higher!

> *Fifth dance lesson.*

From left: Jonathan Chan as Teacher Chen Yuen, Edric Hong as Teacher Chen Lueng and John Gomez Goodway as Li Cunxin in Monkey Baa's 2016 production. (Photo: Heidrun Löhr)

TEACHER GAO *enters.*

CUNXIN *is late getting to the barre.*

TEACHER GAO: You're late. You've been here for seven months. You should know better by term three that lateness is not tolerated.

CUNXIN: Yes. Teacher Gao. Sorry, Teacher Gao.

TEACHER GAO: Leg up on the barre.

As CUNXIN *puts his leg up:*

This term we're refining our Beijing Opera movement. Take your positions. Keep your legs straight. Bend your body forward. Try to touch your head to your toes. [*To* CUNXIN] You. The boy with the brainless big head. Stay down. Don't get up until I tell you so. It is Madame Mao's wish that you don't just grow up to be dancers, but Revolutionary Guards. Your weapon is your art. The expectation is enormous. The hurdle is high. But what you are assigned to do is glorious!

CUNXIN *grabs his hamstring. He is in excruciating pain but does not make a sound.*

Scene Nine

Under a willow. Just before dawn.

CUNXIN *has his blanket. He is alone and homesick. He tries to create a movement piece, repeating a ritual that he has done earlier with his mother. He is visibly upset, crying.*

We hear a stick break and CUNXIN *freezes. He gets up very slowly to go around the willow tree as* WANG LU JUN *comes around the other way. They both scream.*

CUNXIN: Ah!

WANG LU JUN: Ah! What are you doing out here? It's dark.

CUNXIN: What are you doing here?

They see a light switch on in the distance.

BOTH: [*together*] Teacher Gao!

They both dive under the blanket. We hear a cough and then a door close. **CUNXIN** *and* **WANG LU JUN** *both slowly come up out from under the blanket.*

WANG LU JUN: That was close. My name's Wang Lu Jun.

WANG LU JUN *gives* **CUNXIN** *a sweet.*

CUNXIN: I know who you are. Everyone calls you 'The Bandit'. You do those amazing double flying legs. I'm Cunxin from Shandong Provence.

WANG LU JUN: I'm from Shandong Provence too!

CUNXIN: What are you doing out here?

WANG LU JUN: I've been ordered to write three self-criticisms. All I did was buy ten fen worth of sweets.

CUNXIN: I've written many self-criticisms.

WANG LU JUN: Really. Do you want to write another?

CUNXIN: The idea is that you write it.

WANG LU JUN: What am I going to write?

CUNXIN: Well … the ten fen you spent on sweets could have saved someone from starvation.

WANG LU JUN: Good point. Good point.

CUNXIN: Your selfish action could corrupt your mind.

WANG LU JUN: Really?

CUNXIN: Yes.

WANG LU JUN: No?

CUNXIN: Yes. See, it's started already. And thirdly, if you keep buying sweets, you cannot concentrate on your studies and you won't be able to serve in Chairman Mao's revolution anymore.

WANG LU JUN: You're good.

CUNXIN: Well, it's true.

WANG LU JUN: Yes. It is.

> **WANG LU JUN** *offers* **CUNXIN** *another sweet.*
>
> *We hear the sound of a morning bird.*

CUNXIN: Come on, let's go back before we get caught.

> *Both exit.*

Scene Ten

Coming home. Summer.

We hear a steam train. We see steam. In the distant background we see someone on a bicycle coming through the steam.

CUNXIN *appears through the steam, holding a small suitcase and his blanket.*

CUNFAR *calls out from the bike, dinging its bell.*

CUNFAR: Sixth Brother! Sixth Brother. Cunxin!

> **CUNFAR** *gets off the bike and they give each other a big hug.*
>
> *They pick up the bike and begin to walk/dinky ride home.*

CUNXIN: Cunfar! Fifth Brother.

CUNFAR: I've missed you. Look how white your skin is. And look how fat you've got.

CUNXIN: I've missed you, too.

CUNFAR: So tell me, tell me. What is Beijing like? Tell me about the Great Wall, the glorious Tiananmen Square? Have you seen Chairman Mao?

CUNXIN: No, but Madame Mao came to our school and spoke to us.

CUNFAR: Oh, you are lucky, indeed, indeed.

CUNXIN: But I hate dancing. The teachers are mean. They shout at us all the time.

CUNFAR: What are you talking about?

CUNXIN: I just want to come home.

CUNFAR: Cunxin, you don't want my life. This is my first year working in the fields and I hate it already.

CUNXIN: But I'm no good at dancing. My exam results are bad. I think I've failed.

CUNFAR: Then work harder. You can't fail. And don't tell our Niang and Dia about your homesickness. Speak only of the good things about Beijing. I bet you haven't gone to bed with an empty stomach all year.

They are nearing the village. We hear the villagers [UNCLE & AUNTY] *call out.*

UNCLE: Welcome home, Cunxin. Look at the colour of his skin!

AUNTY: Look how fat he's got. Did they bind your feet? Can you walk?

CUNXIN: No, they didn't bind my feet, Fourth Aunty. I can walk.

UNCLE: Come on, teach us some dancing.

CUNXIN: Later, Fourth Uncle.

CUNFAR: Don't forget. Only good things about Beijing.

DIA enters. CUNFAR exits with his bike.

DIA: You're back.

CUNXIN: Dia!

DIA and CUNXIN hug.

NIANG enters.

CUNXIN: Niang!

NIANG: My son. My son. How I missed you. How I missed you. I nearly died missing you.

> NIANG *and* CUNXIN *hug.* CUNXIN *gives* DIA *three yuan.*

CUNXIN: Here, Dia, I saved this money for you. Three yuan.

DIA: Why didn't you buy something for yourself in Beijing?

CUNXIN: I thought it would help the family.

NIANG: Did you miss your home?

CUNXIN: No. Not too much … only a little.

> CUNXIN *hands some sweets to* NIANG.

Here, these sweets are for you, Niang.

NIANG: This is too much.

DIA: How much did they cost?

CUNXIN: Ten fen.

> DIA *shakes his head.*

I know how much you like sweets.

DIA: And your exam results?

> CUNXIN *hands* DIA *an envelope with his exam results.*

> DIA *puts the envelope in his pocket and exits.*

NIANG: Come. I'm making your favourite—dumplings. And you can tell me all about Beijing.

> *As* NIANG *exits,* CUNXIN *practices some of what he has learnt in Beijing.*

Scene Eleven

In the village. A month has passed.

CUNXIN *enters the compound. Villagers* [UNCLE *&* AUNTY] *appear.*

UNCLE: Cunxin, please, please, one last lesson before you go back to Beijing.

CUNXIN: Next holidays, Fourth Uncle.

AUNTY: Come on, Cunxin. One last lesson?

CUNXIN: Alright, Fourth Aunty, one last lesson. I will teach you a Beijing Opera movement exercise. Alright, let's put your legs on the windowsills.

UNCLE: There's no windowsill.

CUNXIN: No windowsill? Oh, okay, Aunty, use Fourth Uncle then. Come on.

> **AUNTY** *struggles to balance, using* **UNCLE** *as a windowsill.*

Keep your legs straight. Bend your body forward. Try to touch your head to your toes.

AUNTY: Ow ow ow.

> *They exit laughing.*

CUNXIN: Where are you going? Fourth Aunty, we're just getting started.

> **DIA** *enters, carrying* **CUNXIN**'s *string sack.* **NIANG** *enters with a small bag of dried yams, and his blanket.*

DIA: Come on, Sixth Son. It is time.

NIANG: I cannot believe it has been one month already, my son.

> **DIA** *hands* **CUNXIN** *something concealed in piece of newspaper.* **CUNXIN** *pulls out the most beautiful royal blue fountain pen from the newspaper.*

DIA: I hope you will use this pen every day. And every time you use it, you will remember your parents and our expectations of you. I don't know what grades your classmates have received, but I hope you will come home with better grades next year. Don't let us down. Let us be proud.

DIA *exits.*

NIANG: Here are some dried yams.

CUNXIN: No, Niang, I get plenty to eat at the academy.

NIANG: Take it, for the train.

CUNXIN: I wish I could stay here forever.

NIANG: You're the lucky one. Become someone other than a peasant boy. Don't look back.

> **NIANG** *gives* **CUNXIN** *his blanket, hugs him tightly, then exits.*

Scene Twelve

Beijing Dance Academy. We hear the ballet school's bell. We hear the piano from the classroom. The new teacher, **TEACHER XIAO,** *enters.*

CUNXIN *struggles with a pirouette.*

CUNXIN: It's no good. It's no good, Teacher Xiao. I'm just no good at it. I can't get it. I will never get this.

TEACHER XIAO: I have watched you over the past year and a half. I have no doubt that you have the inner strength to become a special dancer. Again.

> **CUNXIN** *tries again and fails.*

CUNXIN: I can't find my balance.

TEACHER XIAO: Find your centre. Again.

> **CUNXIN** *tries again and fails yet again.*

Cunxin, nothing is impossible for a determined human being. Find your centre. Again.

> **CUNXIN** *almost falls over.*

CUNXIN: I can't do it, Teacher Xiao.

TEACHER XIAO: Cunxin, I see in you a light I see in no other. You have the ability to be one of the best dancers in the world.

As **TEACHER XIAO** *tells the following story,* **CUNXIN** *lights his candle and begins to reflect the rhythm and sentiment of the story in dance. This could be performed as a slow repetitive action of* **CUNXIN** *learning the process of pirouette.*

Once, in the emperor's palace, there was a young guard. He wanted to be, above all things, the best bow shooter in the land. One day, he went to the finest archer and demanded, 'Master, teach me'. 'No,' said the master.

The following day, the guard returned and asked again, 'Master, will you teach me?' But the master again said no.

For a whole year the young guard came back day after day, week after week, month after month, but still the master said no.

As the days passed, the guard was filled with a growing humility, but he was determined that the master would teach him. The master finally said, 'Yes. Now you are ready to learn.'

The master instructed the young guard to pick up the bow and arrow. But the bow was too heavy. The young guard pleaded with the master, 'When can I shoot the arrow?' The master replied, 'When you can hold the bow lightly above your head. Light as a feather.'

And so day after day the young guard practised holding the heavy bow above his head. Until one day the bow felt as light as a feather.

Next the master asked, 'Can you see that willow tree in the distance?' 'Yes.' 'Can you see the spider in the willow tree?' 'No.' 'Focus on the tree, one eye at a time … and you will see the spider.'

Jonathan Chan (left) as Teacher Xiao and John Gomez Goodway as Li Cunxin in Monkey Baa's 2016 production. (Photo: Heidrun Löhr)

So day after day the young guard focused his eyes one at a time on the willow tree, until eventually … he saw the spider, there in the willow tree, as big as his hand.

'Now,' the master said, 'you are ready to shoot the arrow'.

Scene Thirteen

Beijing Dance Academy. **CUNXIN** *practises by candlelight.*

TEACHER GAO *enters and observes him from the shadows.*

TEACHER GAO: I should have guessed. It's you, the boy with the brainless big head.

CUNXIN: I'm sorry, Teacher Gao.

TEACHER GAO: What are you doing up at this hour of the night?

CUNXIN: I'm practising.

TEACHER GAO: Practising? So the daily routine with your fellow students isn't enough for you? You see yourself above them. Do you?

CUNXIN: No. No.

TEACHER GAO: The peasant thinks he's a prince, does he?

CUNXIN: No, I was practising, Teacher Gao.

TEACHER GAO: Get back to your dormitory.

> **CUNXIN** *picks up the candle and, as* **TEACHER GAO** *goes to leave,* **CUNXIN** *stops her.*

CUNXIN: Teacher Gao?

TEACHER GAO: What?

CUNXIN: I don't like you calling me the boy with the brainless big head. I know I wasn't good in your classes when I first arrived, but after all these years my attitude has changed. I want to be a good dancer. I hope you'll give me a chance.

TEACHER GAO takes the candle off CUNXIN. She blows it out and exits.

Scene Fourteen

Beijing Dance Academy. Spring.

A dance class is in progress with TEACHER XIAO. CUNXIN and other students are present. We hear the piano.

TEACHER XIAO: One, two, three, open four, five, six, turn seven, close eight. And one, two, three, open four, five, six, turn seven, close eight.

> BEN STEVENSON *enters.*

Mr Ben! [*Continuing with the lesson*] Open four, five, six, turn seven, close eight. That will be all for today. Thank you. [*To* BEN] Welcome, Mr Ben. We are honoured to have you here.

BEN: Good to be here again, Teacher Xiao. Thank you for allowing me to observe your class.

> *The class ends.*

TEACHER XIAO: Cunxin. Good work.

CUNXIN: *Xie xie.* Thank you, Teacher Xiao.

TEACHER XIAO: Mr Ben Stevenson, I would like to introduce you to Li Cunxin. Li Cunxin, Mr Ben Stevenson. Mr Ben is the ballet master from the Houston Ballet in America.

CUNXIN: Yes. *Ni hao.*

> CUNXIN *nods.*

BEN: *Ni hao.* I am very pleased to meet you, Cunxin. I am very impressed with your technique.

CUNXIN: *Xie xie.* Thank you.

BEN: Your strength is incredible. Your balance … exciting, Cunxin.

CUNXIN: *Xie xie*. Thank you, thank you.

BEN: Cunxin, I'd like to make you an offer. Would you like to come to America and study ballet with my company, the Houston Ballet?

CUNXIN: America? Me?

TEACHER XIAO: Yes you, Cunxin.

BEN: Please consider this opportunity.

CUNXIN: *Xie xie*. Thank you.

BEN: You're very welcome.

CUNXIN: *Xie xie*. Thank you. Thank you.

> **BEN** *exits*.

I don't believe it. I don't believe it.

TEACHER XIAO: It's an amazing offer from the Houston Ballet. I am so proud of you. It will be wonderful for you to study with Mr Ben. You deserve this.

CUNXIN: America … America! When do we leave?

TEACHER XIAO: Cunxin, I will not be coming. The Chinese Consulate in Houston will meet you at the airport and will look after you.

CUNXIN: But you're my teacher. You made me like ballet. Without you I would never have been given this opportunity.

TEACHER XIAO: Cunxin, if you continue to work in the same way, I have no doubt that one day you will become one of the world's greatest ballet dancers.

Scene Fifteen

In the village / Beijing Dance Academy.

We hear the village loudspeaker making an announcement: 'Li family, to the commune phone, call from Beijing. Li family, call from Beijing.'

CUNXIN *and* **CUNFAR** *talk together by phone.*

CUNXIN: *Wei?* Cunfar?

CUNFAR: *Wei?* Cunxin?

CUNFAR: Is that you, Fifth Brother?

CUNFAR: Yes it is. What's wrong?

CUNXIN: I'm going to America for six months.

CUNFAR: What? It's a bad line. What? America? You're joking.

CUNXIN: No, I'm not joking. I'm going to America to study ballet.

CUNFAR: My brother is going to America! I can't believe this! America! My brother is going to America. I hear everyone has cars, and everyone carries guns. If they don't like you, they'll just shoot you. Here is our Niang … my brother is going to America!

> **NIANG** *runs onstage, calling Cunxin's name. She takes the phone from* **CUNFAR**.

NIANG: Cunxin. My son.

CUNXIN: Niang, how are you?

NIANG: Are you really going to America?

CUNXIN: Yes. I'm leaving in a few days.

NIANG: Why didn't you tell us earlier? I could have sent you some dried yams to take on the road.

CUNXIN: I'm going on an aeroplane.

NIANG: On an aeroplane? *Wo de tian na!* How unthinkable! My son

32

is going to fly on an aeroplane.

CUNXIN: I've met an American dance teacher. Ben Stevenson.

NIANG: Be careful. Stay away from those evil people in America.

CUNXIN: Ben seems very nice. And the Chinese Consul will be there. They'll look after me, Niang. Don't worry.

NIANG: But those foreigners are wild. They are different from us.

CUNXIN: I will be alright, Niang.

NIANG: My sixth son is going to America … on an aeroplane. My heart is bursting with pride.

Scene Sixteen

Houston International Airport.

We can hear planes landing, airport ambience.

A recorded announcement comes over a loudspeaker: 'Ladies and gentlemen. Welcome to Houston International Airport. China Airways Flight 675 from Beijing has arrived at Gate 15. Flight from Beijing disembarking at Gate 15.'

We see CUNXIN *enter the gate lounge. He looks disorientated and is reading his Chinese/English dictionary.*

BEN *and* CONSUL ZHANG *(pronounced: Jung) both enter hurriedly.*

BEN: Cunxin! *Ni hao. Ni hao,* Cunxin!

CUNXIN: Mr Ben!

BEN: Welcome to America. Cunxin, I'd like you to meet Consul Zhang, from the Chinese Consulate here in Texas.

CUNXIN: *Zhang lingshi nin hao.*

> CUNXIN *and* CONSUL ZHANG *shake hands and share a greeting in Mandarin.*

33

CLARE DUNCAN enters, hurriedly, out of breath, carrying a cowboy hat, a gift for CUNXIN.

CLARE: That parking lot was so full. [*Noticing* CONSUL ZHANG] Oh, Consul Zhang. So very lovely to see you again.

CONSUL ZHANG: Mrs Duncan.

BEN: Cunxin, this is Clare Duncan, President of the Houston Ballet.

CLARE: For you.

She puts the cowboy hat on CUNXIN's head.

We're so privileged to have you here at the Houston Ballet.

CUNXIN: *Xie xie.*

CLARE: How was your flight?

CUNXIN: My first time in an aeroplane.

CLARE: Oh, honey. That is precious.

CUNXIN: *Xie xie.*

CLARE: Ben's told us what a fabulous dancer you are.

CUNXIN: *Xie xie.*

CLARE: You've travelled halfway across the world.

CUNXIN: America is very green.

CLARE notices CUNXIN's Chairman Mao pin.

CLARE: Oh, what's that pin?

CUNXIN: Our beloved Chairman Mao.

CLARE: Oh, that's so cute. You must be so tired, Mr Cunxin.

BEN: It's Cunxin, and Li is his surname.

CLARE: Oh, I'm so sorry, Mr Li.

BEN: Do you mind if people call you Li?

CUNXIN: Li? It's okay. Li.

CLARE: Oh good. We're gonna get on like a house on fire, Li.

CUNXIN: House on fire?

BEN: It's an expression. Don't worry. I can't wait to get you to the studio and introduce you to the company.

CLARE: I'll go and bring the car around.

BEN: Let's get your other bags at the carousel.

> **BEN** and **CLARE** go ahead while **CONSUL ZHANG** and
> **CUNXIN** remain.

CONSUL ZHANG: Cunxin, a word.

> **CUNXIN** takes off his cowboy hat.

CUNXIN: Yes, Consul Zhang.

CONSUL ZHANG: These foreigners … they're different from us.

CUNXIN: Yes, very different.

CONSUL ZHANG: They're not to be trusted. You are representing China, and when you return home we expect you to have made us proud.

CUNXIN: I will work very hard.

CONSUL ZHANG: Remember you are a Chinese citizen. You follow Chinese laws, not American laws. *Ni bu hui tian mafan ba.* Li Cunxin, you won't cause trouble now, will you?

CUNXIN: Yes, Consul Zhang.

Scene Seventeen

Houston Ballet School. We hear a piano.

In this scene we see different sequences in preparation for a show—
The Nutcracker. *We see* **CUNXIN** *and a female dancer work through the following sequences, laughing and enjoying both the classes and each other's company.*

BEN *is conducting a warm-up in the style of American dancer and choreographer Martha Graham, possibly with a burst of modern music too, such as Gershwin.*

35

BEN: And one, two, three, four, five, six, seven, eight. Suspend. Roll down. Flat back. Drop your weight. Thank you, that's enough. Welcome, Li, welcome.

A rehearsal.

Move in to the centre. Look at each other. Deeper in your pliés. Lengthen in your arms. Shoulders down. Travel. Travel. Make sure you look at each other. Lovely.

Preparation for a performance. During the following, **CONSUL ZHANG** *appears and observes* **CUNXIN**.

Let's move in to rehearsals. Act Two. Stop there. I need you to get down lower and flick it in his face. Now you need to lean back. Lean more … more … more. That's it. Now, you need to ask for her permission. Good. Good, now continue.

Scene Eighteen

The Chinese Consulate office / Dance of defection.

We hear a jingle: 'Radio Houston, connecting you with the arts, 96.5'.

We are in the Consul's office. As a recorded interview is heard, **CUNXIN** *enters with* **CONSUL ZHANG***, who places a seat in the middle of the stark room. He beckons* **CUNXIN** *to sit in the chair.* **CUNXIN** *appears relaxed as they listen to the following radio interview between* **JANICE** *and* **BEN**.

JANICE: [*voiceover*] Hi, folks, and welcome back to the Arts Hour. We are delighted to have in the studio today Artistic Director of Houston Ballet, Ben Stevenson. So, Ben, what exciting things are happening at the Ballet?

BEN: [*voiceover*] We've had a very successful season, Janice, and we are hoping our visiting artist from China, Li Cunxin, will join us on our international tour next year.

JANICE: [*voiceover*] Fantastic. Li has been dazzling audiences for how long now?

BEN: [*voiceover*] About six months.

JANICE: [*voiceover*] Critics have hailed Li Cunxin, the young dancer, as the next Baryshnikov.

> **CONSUL ZHANG** *indicates for the tape recorder to be switched off.*

CONSUL ZHANG: We here at the Consulate are keen to hear your plans. So what are you hoping to do, Cunxin? Are you hoping to be the next Baryshnikov?

CUNXIN: Well, now that you—

CONSUL ZHANG: He was a traitor.

> **GUARDS** *appear and begin slowly circling* **CUNXIN**, *as the interrogation continues.*

CUNXIN: No, Consul Zhang. But an international tour would be—

CONSUL ZHANG: You don't dance for the world. You dance for China. We don't want to lose our star dancer.

CUNXIN: But Consul Zhang, it would be such an opportunity for me—

CONSUL ZHANG: You are going back to China.

CUNXIN: But—

CONSUL ZHANG: We have the power to do anything that we want with you.

CUNXIN: But Consul Zhang—

CONSUL ZHANG: The answer is no. These foreigners are not your friends. We here at the Consulate are your friends. China is looking forward to your return.

> **CUNXIN** *is silent.*

Think of your parents, Li Cunxin, and all your brothers back home. Think of how proud they will be of you, when you return.

CUNXIN: I don't want to return to China.

CONSUL ZHANG: You don't decide. The Chinese government decides. *Ni bu hui tian mafan ba?* [Li Cunxin, you won't cause trouble now, will you?]

CUNXIN: I don't want to go back.

> As **CUNXIN** *tries to get up from the chair, the* **GUARDS** *close in and try to restrain him in a movement sequence—the dance of defection.*
>
> **CUNXIN** *manages to free himself of the* **GUARDS** *and is back on stage at the Houston Ballet in real-time. During the following movement sequence we begin to hear* **NIANG** *and* **DIA**'s *voices echoing their aspirations for their son from his earlier life. He also hears the chanting from his village school in Shandong.*

DIA: [*voiceover*] Cunxin, you need to feel the current of the wind, like a bird, go with the current of the wind.

NIANG: [*voiceover*] Become someone other than a peasant boy. You have your secret dreams. Follow them.

STUDENTS: [*voiceover*] Long live Chairman Mao, I love Chairman Mao.

Scene Nineteen

Houston, Texas. We are back in real-time at the beginning of our story. We hear the foyer bells indicating the show is about to begin.

We hear a voiceover making the audience announcement: 'Ladies and gentlemen, in tonight's performance of Houston Ballet's The Nutcracker, *the role of the Prince will be danced by Li Cunxin.'*

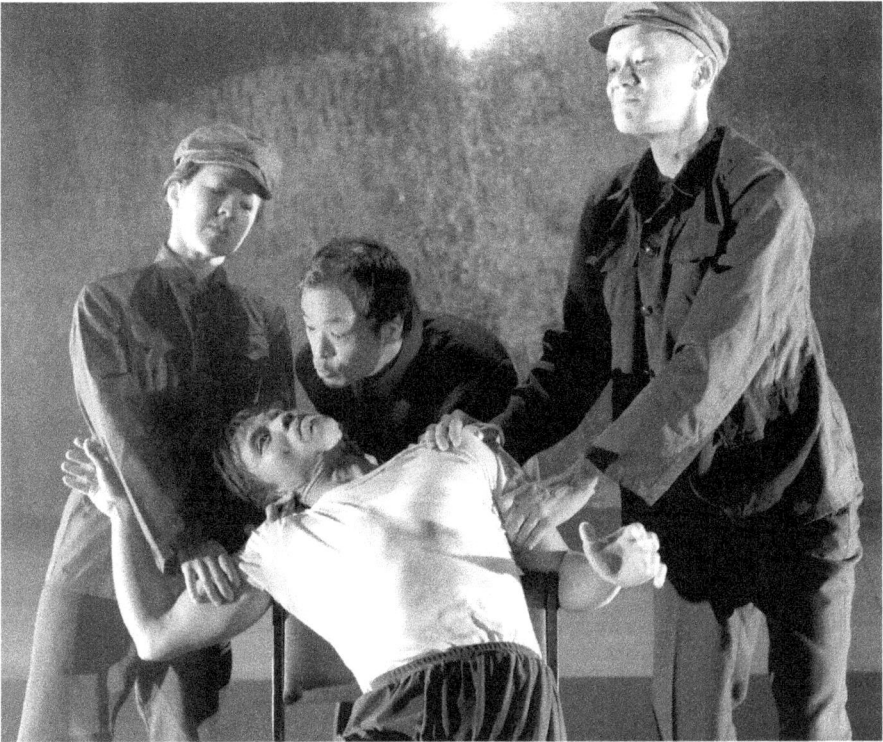

From left: Jenevieve Chang as a Guard, John Gomez Goodway (foreground) as Li Cunxin, Jonathan Chan as Consul Zhang and Edric Hong as a Guard in Monkey Baa's 2016 production. (Photo: Heidrun Löhr)

The **STAGE MANAGER** *enters.*

STAGE MANAGER: [*on his mic*] I'm still waiting for clearance. [*To* **CUNXIN**] Li, your parents have finally arrived.

CUNXIN: Where are they sitting?

STAGE MANAGER: [*on his mic*] Where are they seated? The parents? [*To* **CUNXIN**] Front row, centre.

CUNXIN: I haven't seen my Niang and my Dia in six years.

STAGE MANAGER: They'll be so proud. We have FOH clearance. Li, are you ready? [*On his mic*] Ladies and gentlemen of the company, please stand by. [*To* **CUNXIN**] You are the Prince.

We hear the opening bars of 'The Nutcracker Suite'.

CUNXIN *moves towards towards the Houston Ballet audience, preparing to dance.*

We see an image of **LI CUNXIN** *dancing on the screen. As the footage begins,* **NIANG** *and* **DIA** *appear and watch their son's ballet prowess in awe and with immense pride.*

We hear **LI CUNXIN***'s voice:*

CUNXIN: [*voiceover*] The little frog did get out of the well. My dreams did come true. After all these years I'd become one of the world's greatest dancers. But I'll never forget that small boy flying his kite in the remote village in China.

An image of the kite appears and dances with the footage of **LI CUNXIN** *dancing. We hear the gentle flapping of the kite in the wind as the lights fade.*

THE END

Teachers' Notes

CONTENTS

ABOUT THE TEXT

The Peasant Prince is a stage adaptation of the children's picture book of the same name by Li Cunxin. This picture book is a retelling of Cunxin's autobiography, *Mao's Last Dancer*. Anne Spudvilas' beautiful illustrations inspired much of the costume and set design for the Monkey Baa stage production, especially the use of charcoal and watercolours.

The Peasant Prince was brought to Monkey Baa's attention during a student workshop in a small school in Far North Queensland, Australia. The workshop tutor had asked the students to re-enact a scene from their favourite picture book, using only movement—no words. The tutor recognised the scene … it was somehow familiar. The miming captured a boy performing stretches and dance steps for stern-looking adults. Then the boy was taken away from his family. After the performance, the students expressed their admiration for the book and for Li Cunxin's story. This sparked Monkey Baa's interest in an adaption of the story for the stage.

Li Cunxin's story of his remarkable life is celebrated as an example of the power of hope, hard work and resilience—that a person can bring their dreams and ambitions to reality through hard work and a steadfast resolution to never give up.

ACKNOWLEDGEMENTS

Thanks must go to: Li Cunxin and Anne Spudvilas; Monkey Baa's Education Consultant, Rachel Perry; Monkey Baa Teaching Artists for the 2016 tour of *The Peasant Prince* Belinda Hoare, Luke Kerridge, David Lynch and Bali Padda; thank you to Kate Walder for the playbuilding ideas in this resource; and a huge thank you to the thousands of students around the nation who participated in a Monkey Baa workshop linked to our production of *The Peasant Prince*.

LINKS TO THE AUSTRALIAN CURRICULUM (v8.2)

ENGLISH

Year 2

- Understand that spoken, visual and written forms of language are different modes of communication with different features and their use varies according to the audience, purpose, context and cultural background (ACELA1460)
- Use interaction skills including initiating topics, making positive statements and voicing disagreement in an appropriate manner, speaking clearly and varying tone, volume and pace appropriately (ACELY1789)
- Rehearse and deliver short presentations on familiar and new topics (ACELY1667)
- Innovate on familiar texts by experimenting with character, setting or plot (ACELT1833)

Year 3

- Draw connections between personal experiences and the worlds of texts, and share responses with others (ACELT1596)
- Discuss how language is used to describe the settings in texts, and explore how the settings shape the events and influence the mood of the narrative (ACELT1599)

Year 4

- Make connections between the ways different authors may represent similar storylines, ideas and relationships (ACELT1602)
- Use metalanguage to describe the effects of ideas, text structures and language features of literary texts (ACELT1604)
- Discuss how authors and illustrators make stories exciting,
- moving and absorbing and hold readers' interest by using various techniques, for example character development and plot tension (ACELT1605)

Year 5

- Plan, rehearse and deliver presentations for defined audiences and purposes incorporating accurate and sequenced content and multimodal elements (ACELY1700)
- Use metalanguage to describe the effects of ideas, text structures and language features on particular audiences (ACELT1795)

Year 6

- Compare texts including media texts that represent ideas and events in different ways, explaining the effects of the different approaches (ACELY1708)
- Plan, rehearse and deliver presentations, selecting and sequencing appropriate content and multimodal elements for defined audiences and purposes, making appropriate choices for modality and emphasis (ACELY1710)
- Create literary texts that adapt or combine aspects of texts students have experienced in innovative ways (ACELT1618)

DRAMA

Year 2

- Explore role and dramatic action in dramatic play, improvisation and process drama (ACADRM027)
- Use voice, facial expression, movement and space to imagine and establish role and situation (ACADRM028)

Year 3-4

- Explore ideas and narrative structures through roles and situations and use empathy in their own improvisations and devised drama (ACADRM031)
- Use voice, body, movement and language to sustain role and relationships and create dramatic action with a sense of time and place (ACADRM032)

Years 5-6

- Explore dramatic action, empathy and space in improvisations, play building and scripted drama to develop characters and situations (ACADRM035)
- Develop skills and techniques of voice and movement to create character, mood and atmosphere and focus dramatic action (ACADRM036)

GENERAL CAPABILITIES and CROSS-CURRICULUM PRIORITIES

- Literacy
- Intercultural understanding
- Ethical understanding
- Personal and social capability
- Critical and creative thinking
- Information and communications technology
- Australia's engagement with Asia

WORKSHOP ACTIVITIES

1: Begin with the Picture Book

Monkey Baa is known for stage adaptations of quality children's literature. The company's creative process begins with the original text, and stays closely aligned with it throughout the adaptation process. The playwrights scoured the source for clues and details.

Firstly, take time to read the visual cues and deduce context. Start with the picture book's visual information:

- Front cover
- Inside cover
- Dedication
- Illustrations

Think about and discuss:

- The materials used in the illustrations
- The repetition of kite and frog motifs at the end of the book
- How the illustrations reflect the book's cultural context

There is in-depth discussion to be had around the colour scheme of the book, and how colour is used to tell the story—to find contrast, and to take the reader on a journey. Note how the colour scheme changes for the final images of the book, when Li is dancing *The Nutcracker*. Compare opinions and record them in the groups.

Who Are the People in This Story?

Without reading any of the text, discern who the characters might be. Split into small groups and look at one double-page spread per group. Discuss. Decide who is in the scene, what the action or story of the scene is, what might have just happened, and what is about to happen. Write down your ideas on a piece of paper. Afterwards, present each group's deductions to the class. This is a great activity as there is no right or wrong at this stage—and it assesses prior learning.

The Title

What does the title mean? Who is the peasant and who is the prince? Are they two different people, or the same person? Use role-play and movement to explore what it is like to pretend to be a peasant. What are the steps between peasant and prince?

The Book

It's time to read the picture book aloud as a group.

2: Creating a Moved Synopsis of the Story

Warm-up: Rubber Chicken

- Shake your right hand eight times

- Shake your left hand eight times
- Shake your right leg eight times
- Shake your left leg eight times
- Repeat this sequence, reducing the amount of shakes by one each time (7, 6, 5, 4, 3, 2, 1)
- Shake your whole body

Mime

Have the class walk around the classroom without talking. Instruct them to do one of the following:
- Stop (stand still on the spot)
- Go (walk)
- Jump (jump once)
- Clap (clap once)

Once good focus is established, announce everything is now opposite: when you say Go, they have to Stop, and so on.

Announce the opposites have disappeared. Have the class sit on the floor facing you with their eyes closed. You are going to lead them through a visualisation and a mime. They are going to mime what it is like to be a peasant. Have them imagine details of the scene, such as:
- It is winter
- You live on a farm
- It is snowing outside
- You have a small fire and stove to keep warm
- You eat your meals seated on a mat on a dirt floor
- You have six brothers and sisters
- Your parents work in the fields all day
- For a meal you have a small bowl of rice and some dried yams (which are starchy vegetables, like potatoes)
- You must share the food with your whole family

- Your parents always eat less than the children
- You are still hungry when you finish
- Your walls are covered in newspaper
- You must sleep on the floor on simple bedding, and your brother's feet are always in your face

Give the class some time to mime their interpretation of the above scenario while you describe the features of the scene. Adding some music might enhance their focus, and the atmosphere of the activity.

Bring this mime to a close.

Repeat <u>Rubber Chicken</u> to 'shake off' the mime.

EXTENSION: Repeat the above process but feed in stimuli relating to the abundant wealth, status and riches of a prince. After shaking off this exercise, have the students share their reflections on these contrasting experiences.

Tableaux

Use tableaux to embed the plot of the story and create a synopsis.

Divide the class into eight small groups, and allocate one of the below eight events to each group. Perhaps give them the picture book so they can refer to their page(s).

1. Li's father (Dia) telling him the story of the frog in the well
2. The visit to Li's school by officials of the Chinese Government
3. Li is selected to study at Madame Mao's academy in Beijing
4. Li leaves his family and travels to Beijing
5. Teacher Xiao encourages Li to believe he can succeed
6. Ben from America asks Li to dance with the Houston Ballet
7. Li dances with companies across the world, leaving China permanently
8. Li's parents see him dance *The Nutcracker* and he is reunited with them

Task each group to create one frozen picture that captures this moment. Present each of the eight moments to the class. Then, assemble them into order and run them fluidly together, so the class has a moved synopsis of the whole story. You could film this and have it as an audiovisual reference, perhaps watching it at the start or end of a lesson (or as a reward).

EXTENSION: Create transitions between each group's image by emulating cinematic techniques but as live, physical transitions. For example, how can you fade to black on stage? How can you wipe the screen left to right? How can you jump-cut to the next scene, or crossfade? Look at examples of these sorts of cinematic transitions. Name them and describe them. Choose which transition type will be placed between each scene. Work together to stage the cinematic transition between each scene. Run the synopsis again, in order, with your transitions added.

3: Scene Study

Warm-up: Laser Beams

- Have students form pairs, except for one student who goes outside the room.
- Each pair stands opposite each other. They can spread out around the space. They can also be at varying heights. The one thing that is most important is that they must maintain eye contact with each other and remain facing each other. Their eye contact becomes a laser beam.
- Place an object somewhere in the room, surrounded by the laser beams.
- The student who was outside the room enters and needs to work through the obstacle course to get to the object. They need to strategise and think about the best possible way to reach the object without crossing a beam.

- If the student crosses a laser beam, the beam's pair must say 'BZZZ!' If the student crosses three beams, they are out.
- Give turns to other students.

Scene Work

Have a look at the play script. The following scene (pp. 8-9) is about a moment that is NOT in the picture book.

PLAY SCENE

NIANG *pulls a small car out of her pocket and shows it to* **CUNXIN**.

NIANG: Is this your toy car?

>   **CUNXIN** *is silent.*

Get inside. Get inside now!

>   *They move inside.*

Where did you get this toy car?

CUNXIN: I found it, Niang.

NIANG: Where?

CUNXIN: In the street.

NIANG: When?

CUNXIN: Yesterday.

NIANG: Did you steal it?

CUNXIN: No, Niang.

NIANG: You did.

CUNXIN: I didn't …

NIANG: You stole this toy car.

CUNXIN: I didn't …

NIANG: I am ashamed …

CUNXIN: But Niang—

NIANG: I am ashamed of what you have done. Push the windbox.

I have tried to teach all my seven sons never to steal. Push the windbox. You have shamed me …

CUNXIN: Alright.

NIANG: You have shamed your Dia …

CUNXIN: Alright.

NIANG: You have shamed the Li family name.

CUNXIN: Alright, I stole it. But stop yelling at me!

NIANG: Push the windbox! And tomorrow you are going to return this toy.

DIA *enters and overhears* NIANG *and* CUNXIN.

CUNXIN: Why are we so poor?

NIANG: I don't know. We are born with a hopeless fate.

CUNXIN: Don't say that.

NIANG: The gods in heaven won't answer our prayers and even the devil below has abandoned us.

CUNXIN: Don't say that.

NIANG: I'm sorry. I'm sorry we are so poor.

DIA: We may be poor, but no matter how hard life is the Li family always has pride and dignity.

CUNXIN: I'll have enough food for you one day, Niang. I swear.

END SCENE

Discuss:

- Why do you think the play contains this scene?
- What does the scene tell the audience about the story?
- What does the scene add to the story that may not be in the picture book?

Allocate the class into pairs. One student is Li, the other is Niang. Have each pair choose a section of the scene they would like to present to the class. Ensure the pairs consider the setting, and encourage the use of mime to describe props and other objects in the scene.

Before the pairs perform their scenes, ask them to sit in front of the class and be interviewed, in character, about what has happened JUST BEFORE this scene takes place. After they perform the scene, interview them again about what happens JUST AFTER this scene, imagining and improvising the different possibilities and scenarios.

4: Personal Journey

Warm-up: My Bedroom

Place the class into pairs. Person A has 90 seconds to describe their bedroom to person B. Person B must listen carefully and remember as much detail as possible. Once the 90 seconds are up, the pairs swap over—person B describes their room and person A listens. Each partner must then describe the other person's bedroom to the rest of the class, recounting as much detail as possible.

Other topics aside from rooms could be: a family holiday, a favourite meal and how to prepare it, or a memorable story about a celebration. All pairs need to be assigned the same topic, so there is a sense of shared community built around the topic.

Personal Journey

As a class, think about and share knowledge of Li Cunxin's life story. Plot the main biographical events of Li Cunxin's life as a series of bullet points on a piece of paper. Your information sources can include the picture book, the play script, prior knowledge, and other research.

Using the bullet points you have assembled as a class, craft a prose biography of Li's life and career. Establish parameters for this biography, such as length or word count, and define clearly the purpose of the biography.

Next, have the class reflect on their own biography. Have them assemble perhaps ten bullet points about their own life, listing key moments thus far. Have each class member then represent this as a life story, or autobiography, in a format of their choosing. Students may like to incorporate photos in their life story.

Options for the format of their autobiography might include:

- A prose passage
- A photo study with captions
- A video diary
- An artwork or illustration
- An interview
- A TV show ('This Is Your Life'-style) presentation.

Consider the way Li Cunxin shaped his destiny, the transformation he has undergone from being the 'frog at the bottom of the well' to 'the frog at the top of the well'. List the actions that enabled Li to achieve this. List the qualities you perceive in Li, that enabled him to achieve this. Compare ideas and findings as a class.

EXTENSION: What are the alternatives for Li? What if he had rejected the offer of the place at Madame Mao's academy? What if he had stayed in America and not travelled to Australia? Examine the impact of these decisions on Li's fate by imagining, and role-playing, possible alternatives and narratives for Li's story.

5: Propaganda and Politics

The Peasant Prince contains many references to the cultural and political circumstances in China at the time of Li Cunxin's childhood. Many students will need to explore these circumstances in some depth to make them more familiar.

Warm-up: Enemy/Protector

Life in a dictatorship can be very dangerous if you do not agree with the views of the dictator and ruling party. This activity explores what it feels like to have enemies and to have allies.

- Have the class move around the room, at a steady walking pace. No talking.
- Encourage the class to fill all the empty spaces, changing direction and not getting caught going around and around in the same circle.
- Instruct them to choose one person who is a friend to them, an ally. This is their Protector. They must not tell the person they are their Protector. Instruct the class they want to be as close as possible to their Protector at all times. Students walk around the space randomly.
- Pause. Now instruct the class they are going to choose a different person. This person is their Enemy. They need to stay as far away from this person as possible.
- Experiment with trying to stay away from your Enemy and close to your Protector simultaneously. You can also turn up an imaginary magnetic force field that affects how urgently everyone needs to achieve their goal of being closer or further away from their nominated Protector/Enemy.
- At the end of the game, have the class point to their Protector, and then their Enemy, revealing their chosen people.

Propaganda

Research and discuss the Mao regime's use of propaganda. Discuss propaganda more generally—what is it for, and what are its features?

In small groups, you will work together to create a piece of propaganda. This will be in the form of an advertisement that you devise. Select a product—this could be an object, an ideal, or a belief system. Sell the product to a specified audience by performing a 60-second commercial. Be selective in the information you convey, remembering that propaganda by its nature usually emphasises the positives and conceals the negatives. Your ad must contain the following:

- A jingle—a catchy song or chant
- A promise/guarantee—a guaranteed outcome to the user
- A surprise—something must be revealed in the ad that the viewer is not expecting
- A threatened consequence—what is going to happen to the viewer if they do not buy your product?

Rehearse and perform your 60-second ads to the class.

EXTENSION: Can you find examples of modern propaganda?

6: Unplugged Coding

Warm-up: Wink Murder

- Have the class sit on the floor in a circle with their legs crossed. Send someone outside the classroom—this is the Detective.
- Nominate one person to be the Murderer. Explain that the Murderer will lead the rest of the class in a series of movements. The class must follow what the Murderer does, copying their movements—but they must not give away to the Detective the identity of the Murderer. Bring the Detective back in. They get three chances to correctly guess the Murderer.
- Play again, with new Murderers and Detectives.

Coding

Unplugged coding teaches the fundamentals of computer science, whether you have a computer in the classroom or not.

Ask the students what a code is. When you break it down, what is the definition of a code? Coding is the creation of a mapped set of instructions that guide a user to achieving a specific result. We input the code, perform the instructions, and it leads us to a specified outcome.

Students will work together to develop a code that instructs how to perform the five basic positions of ballet.

Find a resource that clearly shows what the five positions are, for both legs and arms. Starting as a whole group to demonstrate, have students volunteer to trial some ideas for First Position at the front of the room. First Position includes these elements:

- Heels together
- Toes apart and wide, in a triangle shape ('turned out')
- Legs straight
- Inner knees and inner thighs close together
- Arms in a curve with elbows bent
- The curved arms form a circle from the shoulders to the fingertips
- Fingertips are not touching
- Neck long and shoulders down away from the ears

Students work together to develop visual and /or physical instructions that guide a user to correctly perform the five basic positions.

7: Cultural Exchange

Warm-up: Gibberish Interpreter

- Have a pair stand in front of the class. These students (Player A and Player B) improvise a short scene, using only gibberish—no recognisable words.
- Have another pair (Player C and Player D) come to the stage and join them, standing on opposite sides of the stage. These students are the interpreters.
- Player A says a gibberish line. Player C interprets this into English. Player B says a gibberish line, and Player D interprets.
- Continue this pattern throughout the scene. This takes some getting used to, especially as the intensity of drama or action in

the scene increases. Keep the scenes short and give parameters of setting, title and/or scenario.

Cultural Exchange Playbuilding

The Peasant Prince traverses Chinese (Eastern) culture, and American (Western) culture. As a class, consider what constitutes 'culture': shared expectations, rituals, symbols, and so on. Consider how culture is expressed through our attitudes, body language, gestures and non-verbal accommodation.

- Have the class spread out and find a quiet spot to sit comfortably and close their eyes.
- Play a selection of music that is from a culture that is unfamiliar to most students—perhaps music from China. You could also choose music that seems to fuse the traditions of more than one culture.
- Have the class quietly listen to the music in its entirety, encouraging them to allow images, memories, colours, ideas to appear to them in their mind's eye.
- Once the music stops, encourage them to quietly form small groups with those nearest them. Each person tells their group what they visualised to the music.
- The groups then select three of these visualisations and use them as the basis for two frozen pictures (tableaux) and one short scene that can contain a maximum of five words. Give the class about ten minutes to prepare.
- Share the scenes with the rest of the class.

EXTENSION: Look through the play script for *The Peasant Prince*, finding vocabulary that is unfamiliar. As a class, make a list of these words. Look up the definitions or translations, and share discoveries. If students speak languages other than English, add translations to the list in these languages as well. Speak the words in new languages aloud as a whole class, with students taking turns to instruct others in pronunciation.

8: Symbolic Expression: Using movement to tell the story

Warm-up: A Prop and What it's NOT!

The class stands in a circle. The playing space is in the centre of the circle. This is a rolling improvisation, with each player stepping into the circle when they are ready to have their turn. Place a simple prop into the centre of the circle. This could be a blanket, a kite, a pair of chopsticks, or a pair of ballet shoes. (All of these suggestions are pertinent to *The Peasant Prince*. The game works just as well with any object, such as a water bottle or a balloon.) The objective of the activity is to enter the space, pick up the object and immediately endow the object as being something it is not.

For example, let's say you have a blanket in the centre. The first student enters the circle and pretends the blanket is a dancing partner. They don't tell the rest of the class their choice—they simply pick up the blanket, and start dancing with it in a ballroom-hold position with their arms.

Or, they might decide the blanket is a pizza base, so they knead it, flip it, roll it out, place toppings on it and put it in the oven. At the end of their improvising, they can leave the blanket in the middle and the next person can enter to transform the prop into something totally different.

This is a great activity for encouraging clear and imaginative physical (non-verbal) offers.

Symbolic Expression of the Story

This activity will give students a chance to use movement to enhance their telling of Li Cunxin's story. It is enriching to add a musical soundtrack to underscore their movement work when they perform their pieces for the class. For background, read the notes (pp. 48-51) about the use of movement as a storytelling device in Monkey Baa's production of *The Peasant Prince*.

Firstly, identify sequences the class will retell through movement. Here is a list of suggestions:

- Li playing with the kite with his father
- Li and his fellow students being tested for strength and flexibility by the visiting officials, and Li being chosen
- Li saying goodbye to his parents before he travels to Beijing
- Li arriving in Beijing for the first time
- Li practising his ballet moves and working hard, and his progress over time
- Li travelling to America and meeting people there, and dancing with the Houston Ballet

With the class divided into small groups, allocate a sequence from the list above (or of your own choosing) to each group. Ask them to identify the beginning, middle and end steps of this sequence. Ask them to identify the climactic point of the action: the most heightened emotional moment in the sequence. The students can then create a freeze-frame for the beginning, middle and end, plus the climactic moment. Have them run these freeze-frames with musical accompaniment several times.

Then, have them work on filling in the transition steps between each freeze-frame. Instruct the students their whole movement piece should be three minutes long.

Students can use elements of drama as a guide to approaching their movement task. Consider the use of gesture, and the use of repetitive gestures. There are some incredible movement sequences depicted in video footage from physical theatre companies such as DV8, a UK physical theatre company of great renown.

As an extension to this, film the groups' movement pieces. In the editing process, should you have access to software for video editing, add music, sound effects, and transition effects such as crossfading.

Movement/Mime

In the original production of *The Peasant Prince*, movement and mime were used as storytelling devices. In order to build movement for these sections, the actors were given a series of tasks. A movement task is simply a physical activity that has a beginning, a middle and an end.

As a motif of Niang's love, the blanket was used symbolically several times throughout the production to tell the story.

For example, in scene three (pp. 7-10) Niang and Cunxin argue over a toy car. By the end of the dialogue the argument remains unresolved. After the argument, and through a series of movements, we see Niang use the blanket to care for her son. In each task we see her use the blanket as a wok as she cooks a meal, then lay out the blanket as a map on the floor and serve Cunxin a meal, miming an imaginary ladle, then use the blanket as a towel to dry his hair after bath time, and eventually use the blanket to wrap him and keep him warm at bedtime. Each task is very simply acted out, without dialogue. Together with these tasks we see an emotional change between the characters, particularly Cunxin who is first angry with his mother, then calming down for mealtime, then delighted at bathtime, and eventually giving in to the loving arms of his mother at bedtime.

In scene six (pp. 15-17), Niang uses a handmade blanket as a symbol of her love when she farewells her son. In ritualised movement, developed through task work, Niang gives the blanket to Cunxin, folding it in his arms. As they slowly part, the letting-go of the blanket is symbolic of Niang's release of her son.

In scene nine (pp. 20-22) under the willow tree, Cunxin feels homesick and he brings out the blanket and repeats one of the movements previously seen in the play.

Each of these tasks or movement sections are supported by music—a traditional Chinese lament—which acts as a method of 'binding' together music, movement and emotion in a simple but effective theatrical storytelling device.

ADDITIONAL RESOURCES

Websites

- Monkey Baa Theatre Company: www.monkeybaa.com.au
- Li Cunxin: www.licunxin.com
- Unplugged Coding: https://code.org/curriculum/unplugged

Publications

- *The Peasant Prince – The True Story of Mao's Last Dancer*, by Li Cunxin, illustrations by Anne Spudvilas. Penguin, 2007.
- *Mao's Last Dancer*, feature film directed by Bruce Beresford. Great Scott Productions, 2009.

RECOMMENDED PLAYS FOR YOUNG READERS

PETE THE SHEEP

Eva Di Cesare, Sandra Eldridge and Tim McGarry
Based on the picture book by Jackie French and Bruce Whatley

Shaun the Shearer just wants to give smokin' haircuts to sheep; it's his calling. Unfortunately the other shearers on the station don't like Shaun's new-fangled ways – he even has a sheep-sheep instead of a sheep-dog! Cast from his shearing role, Shaun and his partner Pete the Sheep set up their own creative hair salon in town. Before long word is out and all the sheep in town are down for a do, and maybe even the big boys too!

978-1-92500-543-1, also an ebook

THE GRUMPIEST BOY IN THE WORLD

Finegan Kruckemeyer

Zachary wants to be different. So he thinks of all the other places out there – filled with giants, and miniatures, and hairy things, and flying things – places where he would not be middling at all. And so he sets out... to stand out. Winner of the 2014 AWGIE Award for children's theatre.

978-1-92500-542-4, also an ebook

ALICE IN WONDERLAND

Mary Anne Butler

Lewis Carroll's whirling, fantastical masterpiece is faithfully and beautifully recreated as a non-stop, madcap theatrical adventure. This classic kids' tale is now an all-new Australian adaptation by multi award-winning playwright Mary Anne Butler.

978-1-76062-192-6, also an ebook

MASQUERADE
Kate Mulvany, adapted from the picture book by Kit Williams

In a wondrous world of riddles and hidden treasure, bumbling Jack Hare is on a race against time to deliver a message of love from the Moon to the Sun. Far, far away in a world just like ours, a mother cheers her son Joe with the tale of Jack Hare's adventure. But when Jack's mission goes topsy-turvy, Joe and his mum must come to the rescue, and the line between the two worlds becomes blurred.

978-1-92500-584-4, also an ebook

THE BOOK OF EVERYTHING
Richard Tulloch, adapted from the book by Guus Kuijer

Thomas writes down all the interesting things he sees that other people seem to ignore: tropical fish in the canal, a deluge of frogs, the Son of God popping in for a chat… He also writes down his greatest determination: When I grow up, I'm going to be happy. This is a totally magical story about a child learning to act when faced with fear and injustice.

978-0-86819-933-7, also an ebook

HONEY SPOT
Jack Davis

The friendship between an Aboriginal boy and a white girl raises issues of race in a touching story of two families who seem to have nothing in common … until danger strikes, forcing them to face their prejudices. Illustrated by Ellen Jose.

978-0-86819-163-8, also an ebook

www.ingramcontent.com/pod-product-compliance
Lightning Source LLC
Chambersburg PA
CBHW050021090426
42734CB00021B/3372